Aromatherapy   ABC

A-Z with essential oils

Angelica

Angélica

Basil

Albahaca

Chamomile
Manzanilla

Dill

Eneldo

Eucalyptus

Eucalipto

Fennel

Hinojo

Ginger

Jengibre

Helichrysum

Helicriso

Impatiens

Impatiens

Jasmine

Jazmín

Kanuka

Kanuka

Lavender

Lavanda

Myrrh
Mirra

Nutmeg

Nuez moscada

Orange

Naranja

Peppermint

Menta

Quassia

Cuasia

Rosemary

Romero

Sandalwood

Sándalo

Tangerine

Mandarina

Ursinia

Ursinia

Vanilla

Vainilla

Wintergreen

Gaulteria

Xerophyllum

Xerófilo

Ylang ylang

Ylang Ylang

Zinnia

Zinnia

Spanish Pronunciation			
A.	ah	**O.**	oh
B.	beh	**P.**	peh
C.	seh	**Q.**	koo
Ch.	cheh	**R.**	EH-reh
D.	deh	**S.**	EH-reh
E.	eh	**T.**	teh
F.	EH-feg	**U.**	oo
G.	hheh	**V.**	veh
H.	AH-cheh	**W.**	DOH-bleh veh
I.	ee	**X.**	Eh-kees
Ll.	EHL-yeh, EH-yeh	**Y.**	ee GRYEH-gah
M.	EH-meh	**Z.**	SEH-tah, ZEH-tah
N.	EH-neh		
Ñ.	EH-nyeh		